SIAMESE FIGHTING FISH

yearBOOK

Gene A. Lucas, Ph.D.
Edited by Dr. Herbert R. Axelrod

The original version of this book was published by Pet Library, poorly printed and terribly illustrated. It was called **know your bettas**. Inasmuch as the text itself was knowledge at the edge of science, TFH has re-issued the book with the addition of about 100 original illustrations.

The American father of *Betta* genetics was Dr. Myron Gordon. In his laboratory atop the American Museum of Natural History he was assisted by Dr. Herbert R. Axelrod. Together they raised millions of *Betta splendens*, producing many genetic variations which eventually became fixed, acknowledged strains available to hobbyist worldwide. The Japanese enthusiastically greeted these new strains and most of them are still available in Japan.

In the hope that this book will inspire a rekindling of the love for these magnificent fish, TFH is re-issuing it in a modern format.

There is no end to the color and fin varieties possible with *Betta splendens.* Like the Japanese colored carps called KOI, the *Betta splendens* can be produced in magnificent colors and finnage. They are also easier to maintain than koi and while every pet shop will have *Betta splendens*, the Siamese Fighting Fish, in stock, not all have koi.

The original author, Dr. Lucas was not consulted about this new edition (he sold his rights), nor was he able to review the new photos and their captions. Instead TFH relied upon Dr. Herbert R. Axelrod to select and caption the photos.

What are YearBOOKs?

Because keeping Bettas as pets is growing at a rapid pace, information on their selection, care and breeding is vitally needed in the marketplace. Books, the usual way information of this sort is transmitted, can be too slow. Sometimes by the time a book is written and published, the material contained therein is a year or two old...and no new material has been added during that time. Only a book in a magazine form can bring breaking stories and current information. A magazine is streamlined in production, so we have adopted certain magazine publishing techniques in the creation of this yearBOOK. Magazines also can be much cheaper than books because they are supported by advertising. To combine these assets into a great publication, we issued this yearBOOK in both magazine and book format at different prices.

yearBOOKS,INC.
Dr. Herbert R. Axelrod,
Founder & Chairman
Neal Pronek
Chief Editor
Dr. Herbert R. Axelrod
Editor

yearBOOKS are all photo composed, color separated and designed on Scitex equipment in Neptune, N.J. with the following staff:

DIGITAL PRE-PRESS
Michael L. Secord
Supervisor
Robert Onyrscuk
Jose Reyes
Computer Art
Sherise Buhagiar
Patti Escabi
Cynthia Fleureton
Sandra Taylor Gale
Pat Marotta
Joanne Muzyka

Advertising Sales
George Campbell
Chief
Amy Manning
Director
Jennifer Feidt
Coordinator

©yearBOOKS,Inc.
1 TFH Plaza
Neptune, N.J. 07753
Completely manufactured
in Neptune, N.J.
USA

CONTENTS

INTRODUCTION

For most of the 25 years I have kept aquarium fishes, I have been attracted to those that were something more than "just fish." While there are fascinating things about all of them, the kinds that intrigue me most are those that respond to the breeder's touch - that is, species varying so much within themselves that they can lead to the development of new varieties.

For a number of years I devoted my attention to Guppies, but even then I always had a few Bettas around. In graduate school, while working on a Guppy genetic problem, I found myself helping a fellow graduate student propagate Bettas. His real interest, I suspect, was in providing fighting fish for clandestine dormitory bouts.

This magnificent Cornflower Blue (one of the many names given to Bettas which look like this), has a Veil-tail and is sometimes known under the German term *Prachtiges.* Photo by Andre Roth.

This Double-tail Golden Fighter is a 1995 variety. It has a blue dorsal and a golden anal fin. Photo by MP & C Piednoir.

Bettas or Guppies?

Because of local water conditions, we were soon having better luck rearing Bettas than Guppies. My own interest in them was enhanced, I am sure, by their adaptability to, and apparent complete lack of concern for, their unfortunate environment. As we accumulated breeding stock and reared more and more fry I became interested in the many different Bettas turning up in our domestic stock, apparently without reason.

Inadequate information

When I delved into Betta literature I found that most of the scientific studies relating to their genetics and breeding were completed in the 1930's and 1940's.

The fact that Bettas have been continual leaders of aquarium fish popularity stimulated much popular writing about them. The most significant was a series in the now defunct *Aquarium Journal* by the late, highly respected Dr. Myron Gordon. Dr. Gordon was a geneticist with the New York Zoological Society Aquarium.

The modern version of the Cambodia Split-tail (or Double-tail). These are very pretty fish. Photo by MP & C Piednoir.

In the 1960's, at least four more books on Bettas were published. It would seem unnecessary to produce still another but for two important facts. The first is that in every case recent publications contain information that is principally rehashed aquarium lore, or reinterpretation of Gordon's now-aging reviews; the other major consideration, as I see it, is that many rather rigid "rules" have been established which, one would gather, must be followed if one hopes to be a successful Betta breeder. With certain

Modern Split-tail Cambodia Bettas. Photo by Tanaka.

Bettas breed easily. After building a bubble nest, the male wraps his body around the female and squeezes the eggs out of her. Most fishes of the genus *Betta* are mouth brooders and the genus should probably be split into two genera.

This variety is now called the Butterfly Betta, but the first Butterfly Betta was raised by Orville Tutwiler in Florida in 1955. In that fish the red was on the outside edges of the unpaired fins with the inside being clear.

reservations, I consider most of these "laws" unduly restrictive.

Bettas are easy

I hope to show that almost anyone can successfully breed Bettas with little difficulty. I think Betta breeding really is easy. In fact, I believe that any hobbyist wanting to try his hand for the first time with egglaying fishes should start with Bettas. I am confident they offer the best chance for success. Finally, I hope to bring Betta information up to date, noting some exciting research of recent years along with the results of my own studies directed toward genetics and breeding.

A head-on view of a Cambodia Betta. They do have a pugnacious look and they are nasty...but only to fishes of their own kind. Photo by MP & C Piednoir.

THE BETTA'S PLACE IN THE WORLD

Popular writers tell us that Bettas belong to the order Labyrinthici, sub-order Anabantoidea, family Anabantidae. However, in 1963 Liem, by means of careful studies of skeletal structures - especially of the head and branchial (gill and throat) region - convincingly demonstrated that the sub-order Anabantoidea should be reclassified. A new family, Belontiidae, was proposed, with three sub-families. The second of these, the Macropodinae, includes Bettas, Paradise Fish *(Macropodus)*, the Croaking Gourami *(Trichopsis)*, and others.

The generic name *Betta* is credited to Bleeker (1850). In the same year, Cantor described *Macropodus pugnax*, which was later declared to be a species of *Betta*. *Betta splendens* was described by Regan (1910). Dr. Hugh M. Smith, U.S. Commissioner of Fisheries from 1913 to 1922, served as advisor in fisheries to the Siamese government from 1923 to 1935. He studied Siamese fishes of all kinds. He finally

Above: Belontia signata is an air breather related to the Betta. Photo by Edward Taylor.

Below: A hybrid between Betta imbellis and Betta splendens. It seems to be fairly simple to cross several so-called species of the genus Betta.

A male *Betta macrostoma* about to capture two eggs in his mouth. Normally the female spits the eggs she collects into his mouth as well. Photo by Dr. Herbert R. Axelrod

Above: Betta macrostoma was brought into the aquarium trade when Dr. Herbert R. Axelrod collected them in Brunei. They disappeared after a short life in aquaria. This male is in breeding color. This species is a mouthbrooder with the male   carrying the eggs in his mouth. Photo by Dr. Herbert R. Axelrod.

Below: Betta macrostoma, transferring the eggs from the mouth of the female to the mouth of the male. The female assists in gathering the eggs which fall to the bottom of the tank during spawning. Photo by Dr. Herbert R. Axelrod.

authored a monograph on them (U.S. National Museum Bulletin 188, 1945). In it he listed ten references to *Betta splendens* that appeared in scientific papers from 1910 to 1945.

There are several *Betta* species. I will refer only to *Betta splendens* (Regan), commonly known as just "Betta," when I use the term here.

Laboratory Betta

Bettas are found in many scientific laboratories where they are the objects of investigations concerning genetics, physiology, behavior and pharmacology, among other things. While the same might be said for other fishes, few of them are the subjects of such extensive study, and none stirs the imagination as much as that finny gladiator, the Siamese Fighting Fish.

Obtaining Bettas

The usual place to purchase Bettas is your local pet shop. They may also be purchased from specialty breeders. Beautiful specimens are usually available at auction following major shows. I advise purchasing young fish rather than big, fully

Bettas, or Siamese Fighting Fish, have long been laboratory favorites. While they are often used in toxicity studies, their main contribution has been in studying genetics. Weird colors and color combinations occur in random matings as can be seen in the specimen shown above. The pet trade is also very much interested in Siamese Fighting Fish, but for the pet trade deep, rich colors and long flowing fins seems to be the most desirable characteristics. Both photos by Kenjiro Tanaka.

developed ones. This is because Bettas are relatively short-lived. The largest specimens are usually at the peak of their development and can rarely be counted on to survive more than a few months. In fact, they may already be useless as breeders.

It is not easy to determine the age of a Betta. Well cared-for fish may be larger at three months than others are at a year. Fish that display vigorously and build bubblenests in their tanks or jars are likely to breed even if they are small; they are also much more likely to last a while. Bettas are usually bred from three or four months to about a year old; most are deteriorating by the time they are eighteen months old. Few live beyond two years in home aquaria.

Natural range

It is generally - and understandably - supposed that Bettas are Siamese fishes; that is, that they come only from Siam, now known as Thailand. Actually, the extent of their natural range is unknown. With the present unsettled conditions in Southeast Asia, it will continue that way for some time. Quite

A view of Orville Tutwiler's Betta hatchery in 1954. Tutwiler had 250,000 male Bettas in jars at all times. His hatchery was in the Tampa, Florida area.

probably, they should be considered "native" to a much wider area of Southeast Asia than Thailand. I have obtained wild stocks from the Mekong Delta near Saigon, South Vietnam, and from Kuala Lumpur, Malaysia. These areas are distant from one another and neither is very near Thailand.

Undoubtedly artificial cultivation played some part in the wider distribution. (The celebrated mosquito larvae consumption of Bettas would seem to make them welcome imports.) However, a look at some geological characteristics of the area shows that there are no barriers to a wider range. A large part of the South China Sea bottom - roughly from South Vietnam southeast to Borneo, south to Java, northwest to and including Sumatra's eastern part, north past the Malayan Peninsula into Thailand, then east through Cambodia to Vietnam - includes a geological structure called the Sunda platform, part of which is submerged. Geologists feel that this was not always true. They believe that at one time the land area may have been continuous. The Chao Phya and Salween rivers in Thailand and the Mekong, which meanders through Laos, Cambodia and Vietnam, plus many lesser rivers, all flow in a common direction toward the South China Sea. The Mekong in particular has many tributaries along its middle and upper reaches which drain directly from Thailand.

Similarities between fishes of Borneo and Sumatra have been found. This suggests that in the evolutionary past the area was not always separated. If the Sunda platform was ever entirely "dry," the whole area would have been contiguous. Nor are the climatic conditions throughout the area especially variable. I believe that *Betta splendens* has a considerably wider "natural" range than is commonly thought. It should not be considered just a "Siamese" fish.

Although a checklist of the fishes of Vietnam (Kuronuma, 1961) lists only a *Betta pugnax*, I am convinced that the stocks I have from that country are *Betta splendens*. They look and behave like *Betta splendens* and mate readily with domestic stock.

Name confusion

Lacking the many sophisticated techniques used by today's taxonomists, early aquarists and taxonomists often failed to recognize polymorphic variations as such. Therefore, they have Latinized names to every fish that looked different from those already described. The Betta problem was complicated by the fact that a

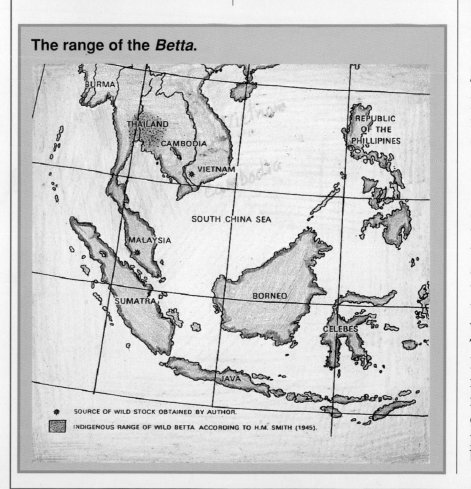

The range of the *Betta*.

SOURCE OF WILD STOCK OBTAINED BY AUTHOR.

INDIGENOUS RANGE OF WILD BETTA ACCORDING TO H.M. SMITH (1945).

number of types based on mutations had been propagated by oriental breeders and exported to such places as Germany, France and the United States.

Eager fanciers were delighted with the "new" Bettas, and a series of new Latinized names soon appeared. A *Betta cambodia* (named for the presumed source), *Betta splendens* var. *longicauda* (referring to the long finnage, specifically the caudal or tailfin), *Betta rubra* (red Betta), *Betta cyano* (blue Betta), *Betta viridens* (green Betta), and others were created. Today hobbyists tend to give their variations more exotic names like "Butterfly," "Golden Cellophane," "Cornflower Blue," "Green-gold," "Fairy-fin," and the like.

I believe that, except for the few rare specimens that occasionally find their way into this country, there is only one *Betta* species commonly found in today's aquarium. It is *Betta splendens* in one of its mutant varieties. It is these mutants that have caused so much confusion.

A relatively newly found *Betta* is this *Betta fasciata*. Though interesting for geneticists, it has little value as an aquarium fish even though it is produced by some fish farms in Florida. Inset: a female *B. fasciata*. Photos by Ed Taylor.

Newly described *Betta albimarginata*. Drawn by John Quinn.

Newly described *Betta channoides*. Drawn by John Quinn.

Side and bottom view of the newly described *Betta chloropharynx*. Drawn by John Quinn.

Betta anabatoides. Photo by Horst Linke.

Betta bellica. Photo by Dr. Herbert R. Axelrod.

Betta pugnax. Photo by E. Roloff.

Betta coccina.
**Photo by Horst
Linke.**

Betta dimidiata.
**Photo by Kenjiro
Tanaka.**

Betta edithae.
**Photo by Horst
Linke.**

Betta livida.
Photo by Dr. J.
Vierke.

Betta foerschi male
in breeding color.
Photo by Horst
Linke.

Betta foerschi
in normal low-
light color.
Photo by Horst
Linke.

Betta imbellis. Two males squaring off for a fight. Photo by Kenjiro Tanaka.

Betta burdigala. Drawn by John Quinn.

The beautiful *Betta smaragdina.* Photo of a breeding male by Hans Joachim Richter.

BETTA SPLENDENS

I think it is necessary for the potential Betta breeder to know a little about normal (wild type) Bettas before he attempts anything beyond superficial breeding. While a knowledge of the anatomy, physiology, reproduction and behavior of the species may not be essential, familiarity with them will lead to a clearer understanding of the variations.

Anatomy

Normal Bettas have bodies of up to two inches, not counting finnage. The body size depends upon diet, condition, age, and, to some extent, inheritance. Average strains tend to produce greatly variable spawns, with "runts" at one extreme and precocious individuals at the other. Extra care and conditioning will give superior results in any case, but selective breeding will produce strains having larger individuals.

Although large size may be a desired factor, size in itself is not as easily studied or developed as some of the other Betta traits that are not so subject to

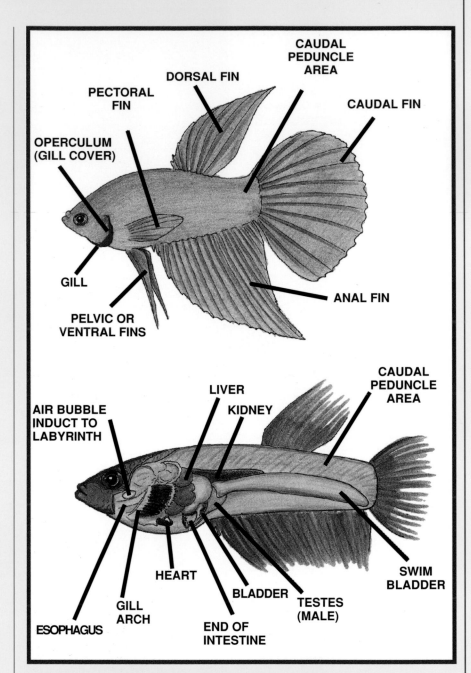

variations caused by external or environmental factors. Therefore, I will disregard size. I will discuss the form and color of wild Bettas, pointing out some of the features that have been discovered in modified form in domestic stocks.

The Betta's body is cylindrical. The head (to the edge of the gill cover) does not reach as far back as a quarter of the body length. Most of the

A male *Betta splendens* during spawning. You can barely see the female behind the male's head. The male is tending the nest as he places eggs into it. Photo by Hans Joachim Richter.

breathing mechanism. This special respiratory modification, called the labyrinth, consists of a pair of irregular passages leading from the mouth cavity up behind the eye, over the gill on either side, and apparently eventually to the swim bladder. A Betta will rise to the surface regularly to gulp air. The air bubbles pass through the labyrinth and provide supplemental oxygen to blood flowing through the vessels lining the membranes of the labyrinth and the gills.

Bettas are not born with this mechanism; it develops by about the tenth day.

Fins

Fins are generally considered as single or paired. The single fins lie in the plane of the midline, and the paired ones to either side of the plane. Bettas have "shoulder" or pectoral girdles and pelvic girdles like most other vertebrates. Although, as in most fishes, this skeletal feature is not so easy to see. The pectoral girdle is located behind the gills and supports two normally colorless "side" or pectoral fins. The pelvic girdle is unusually far forward,

internal organs are located in an abdominal cavity which is relatively small and well forward. More than half (rear) of the body is actually tail (excluding the fin), and is referred to as the caudal peduncle. The fin itself is called the caudal fin. It is not the tail, but it is merely a part of it. Internally, the swim bladder extends all the way into the caudal peduncle.

The only noticeable body variation other than size seems to be a vertical thickening which may include increased numbers of scale rows.

The labyrinth

An important Betta feature is an auxiliary

but near the ventral opening.

The paired fins attached to the pelvic girdle are properly referred to as pelvic or ventral fins. They are much longer, normally bright red and, unfortunately and incorrectly, are often called "pectoral fins" or "feelers," "neckties," and the like. They correspond to the more highly specialized pelvic fins of their relatives, the Gouramis, which *are* used as feelers.

The three remaining fins are the dorsal (back), caudal (tail), and anal (on the bottom, behind the ventral or anal opening). Ichthyologists consider such factors as scale rows, the number of scales along the lateral line, the number of rays of various kinds in fins, etc., extremely important for purposes of identification. These factors are especially important in Bettas, since variation due to genetic abnormality occurs, making individuals easily distinguishable on the

one hand, but species identification uncomfortably confusing on the other.

Usually the dorsal fin has eight to ten rays, the caudal has 12 to 14, and the anal 25 to 30. In wild *Betta splendens*, rays are not "produced." That is, they do not project

The new Peach Cambodia Butterfly Betta. This is incorrectly called the *butterfly* according to the origin of that term because the color should be at the tips of the unpaired fins and not closest to the body. Photo by Kenjiro Tanaka.

noticeably beyond the webbing of the fin as those of many related species do. However, a few of the longest of the rear anal rays may project slightly. Normally the fins of wild Bettas do not extend more than a body width out. This feature is strikingly different from that of most domestic Bettas,

which may be three or four times as long.

Color in Bettas

Since most of the easily observed variations involve color, the normal fish is described here. Note the various elements carefully. They are all subject to variation due to genetic change. I would suggest - oversimplifying, perhaps - that overall differences in appearance are due either to changes of these colors, variations of their amounts and distributions (including possibly their absence), or various combinations of these changes.

Some of the fishes' colors which we see are due to the colors of the tissues themselves, rather than any pigment in the skin. Muscle, connective tissue, blood, food material in the gut, and other things may all be observed to some degree through the semi-transparent skin and muscle. Some fish muscle, especially in young fish, is almost totally transparent, and internal structures are easy to see. In contrast, pigmentation may be so opaque that, no matter how transparent the tissues are, internal structures are still blocked from view.

Pigments

Usually when pigments are present they prevent us from seeing any possible changes of tissue color. So even if it did take place, it is doubtful if the change would be observed.

For the most part, skin pigments are contained in cclls callcd chromatophores. Each type has a special name. For example, a cell containing the dark pigment melanin may be properly called a melanophore. In Bettas, there seem to be four clear-cut pigmentary elements. These are mclanin (black), a ptcrin (red), a lipochrome (yellow), and a "pigment" which may actually be colorless, but which because of physical effects creates strong green and blue "metallic," almost mirrorlike, colors. It is said to be caused by tiny crystals of a substance called guanin in cells called iridophores, iridocytes or guanophores. I refer to color produced by these

Mottled or splashed Cambodia Split-tail. Photo by Kenjiro Tanaka.

Saddle-back Cambodia Black Splash. Photo by Kenjiro Tanaka

Metallic blue in this short-finned *Betta*. Photo by Kenjiro Tanaka.

Two males Siamese Fighting Fish locking jaws during a fight. They will keep at it until their fins are in shreds and one of them gives up. They rarely kill, but they often succumb to infected wounds. Photo by Andre Roth.

Wild Betta behavior

Little has been mentioned about the behavior of wild Bettas.

This is because little is known. Wild Bettas in my tanks have shown a remarkable variation

The upper fish is a fighting male with his gill covers expanded. The lower fish has surrendered and does not raise his gill covers. Photo by Andre Roth.

from the domestic ones. For one thing, they show far less interest in fighting. They seem to be much more aware of what is going on around them. They act quite frightened at sudden disturbances. They go into panicky flight easily, and they are good jumpers. Far and away my greatest problem with them is that they jump - from container to container and to the floor.

My guess is that in the wild they are both shy and retiring. They probably remain pretty much in hiding among leaves in shallow water with only sudden and brief ventures into the open.

Sometimes both fish surrender at the same time and there is no winner...just two fish with tattered fins, too tired to fight any more. Photo by Andre Roth.

MAINTENANCE

Because of their adaptability to poor conditions (as far as oxygen in the water, etc., is concerned), Bettas can survive under circumstances that other aquarium fishes cannot tolerate.

Peaceful Bettas?

As a rule, Bettas can be housed in community aquaria with other fishes, since they are belligerent primarily toward their own kind. Females usually get along well together after they have adjusted to one another. One male and several females can be kept in a tank with other fishes. The trouble begins when two males meet. However, there are exceptions to all of these rules. I have heard several accounts of males being housed together successfully. In a community tank, males are more likely to be sinned against than sinning. Sharp-toothed characins and other small, active fishes frequently nip the fins of the slow-moving Bettas. Occasionally, however, a male Betta will turn rogue, sidling slowly up to smaller fishes. Then, when close enough, he will butt or bite them viciously.

Bettas seem to get along quite well if they grow up together, even beyond the age of sexual maturity. If they are separated from each other, though, and then put back together, they show every sign of having completely forgotten their brothers and sisters. Every fish in the tank is then regarded as a mortal enemy and is immediately challenged to battle. An aggressive look at one elicits an aggressive response from another - and then the fun begins!

Damaged fins heal

Actually, a few healthy tussles are not too harmful. The activity might even be good for wild Bettas, but the long-finned domestic varieties are hardly equipped to win both beauty contests and battles. Since delicate fins damage easily,

Bettas must be kept warm or they will stop feeding, become ill and never spawn. Thermostatically controlled heaters in various wattages are available from your local pet shop. Photo courtesy of Penn Plax.

Dr. Lucas suggests that a *few healthy tussles are not too harmful*. I disagree with him (HRA). While fins do heal, they are never as beautiful as they were before they were ripped and there is always the chance of infection. Photo by Andre Roth.

Bettas never seem to mind what they are kept in. They thrive in close confinement. This is one of the reasons they are such excellent aquarium fish. The biggest problem in maintaining healthy living conditions in these small containers is that conditions can change rapidly. A fish that seems to be doing well one day may be in bad shape the next.

Smaller amounts of water in jars can change temperature rapidly. Therefore, it is best to position containers where they are least likely to be subjected to rapid environmental shifts. Shelves located away from windows or heaters are recommended.

Feeding

Feeding Bettas is not too much of a problem. They will eat almost anything - including chocolate cake! Their favorite natural food is mosquito larvae, but these are not often available. They readily accept almost any conventional fish food, including dry preparations, although they may have to learn to eat them if they have been reared on live foods only. Frozen shrimp,

potential prize winners may be ruined. Young fish heal rapidly, so the injuries themselves present no special problem. As Bettas mature and age, however, they lose the capacity to regenerate fin tissue and pigmentation. The fins may grow back with ragged edges, curved rays, or other lasting impairment. Pigmented areas may be replaced with pigment of another color, or none at all. Of course, there is always the possibility of some fungus or bacterial infection gaining entry at the site of injury. Every injury should be treated with antibiotics.

Housing Bettas

Most Bettas are housed individually. Hobbyists usually select interesting small glass or plastic bowls, or novelty containers for their specimens. These are, as a rule, too expensive for a breeder who has hundreds of fish to house. Therefore, they often are kept in ordinary jars.

Bloodworms can be used as the main diet for Bettas. These frozen items can be found at your local pet shop. Photo courtesy of Hikari.

Keep them clean

Since the labyrinth apparatus relieves the respiratory problem, and their lack of concern over diet makes feeding fairly simple, the biggest Betta problem is usually the maintenance of sanitary conditions in their water. Fecal wastes from the digestive tract, gaseous wastes from respiration and nitrogenous wastes from urine all contribute to the deterioration of their restricted environment, so that disposal of waste products is most important.

Breeders who produce the best fish follow a rigorous routine of water changing. This may

meat and fish bits, paste foods, fruit flies, worms, and other popular fish foods are taken readily and with apparent relish by healthy Bettas. They can and do thrive on limited diets. For proper nutrition, though, a variety should be provided.

Feed only as much as the fish can consume in five minutes, once to several times a day. Clear water and healthy, colorful, alert fish indicate proper and adequate feeding. Underfeeding retards growth and overfeeding (without frequent

cleaning) causes water fouling (indicated by smelly and cloudy water).

An internal canister filter can be placed right into the tank with both filtering and pump areas being completely submerged. Photo courtesy of Penn Plax.

range from merely siphoning off and replacing part of the water to complete water changes and jar washing and sterilization. The frequency of change depends upon several factors: how often the fish are fed; the kind of food; the size of the fish; and the size of the container. The larger the container, the longer it takes for unfavorable conditions to develop. The choice of container is pretty much up to the individual. It is influenced by the

A sure sign of a Betta in distress is when all the fins are clamped tightly closed and they stay that way for more than 5 minutes. Photo by Hans Joachim Richter.

Airpumps are necessary for the operation of many aquarium accessories including airstones, air-driven ornaments and air driven filters. Make sure that the air pump you choose is powerful enough for the size aquarium you have and the specific accessories the pump is driving. Photo courtesy of Penn Plax.

number of fish he wants to keep and the time he has available. I keep fish successfully in quart, half-gallon, and gallon jars. While breeders and potential show fish have their water changed twice weekly, the others are changed only when necessary.

The best indicator of good water conditions is the appearance of the fish. As conditions deteriorate, the fish become less active, show less interest in their neighbors, become pale, clamp fins, and show signs of distress or disease. Healthy fish are active, colorful, and responsive.

COMPETITION

While there is little doubt that the initial interest in Bettas developed because of their natural instinct for fighting, I am sure that the early breeders of fighting fish were also attracted by their beauty. This led logically to the development of such characteristics as fin form, size, and color as objects of the breeders' interest.

Fighting fish have been popular in their native countries for as long as 500 years, if not longer. There is no way to know for sure. They were first seen in Europe in Germany in 1892 and bred a year later in France.

Fighting fishes

When two males meet, they go through a characteristic display; the color intensifies, their gills flare, and they make special swimming movements involving side-by-side motion and wide-spread fins, etc., interrupted suddenly by a rushing attack by one of them. Although their mouths are small, they are armed with tiny teeth which tear off scales and rip delicate webbing from fins. Sometimes the fish lock jaws and roll over and over. Nevertheless, they do have a sense of fair play; they seem willing to allow one another to surface for a gulp of air when necessary.

Fin damage may make swimming difficult, impairing a combatant's ability to continue the fight. The winner is the fish which continues to be the aggressor. The loser shows defeat by losing color and failing to re-engage. He may even assume the vertical

for hours before one admits defeat. The interest among bettors on Betta fights has been described as so intense that even wives were won or lost on wagers.

A more humane form of competition has developed in the USA. This is the showing of Bettas bred for size, form, and color.

Exhibitions

Maximum development of the long, flowing finnage and intensity of the beautiful blue, red,

Let's get on with the fight! Betta fighting is illegal, immoral and disgusting. Join our fight to keep our pets so they can live in peace. Photo by Andre Roth.

banding pattern of the submissive female. Superior fighters, it is claimed, are able to go on

green and other colors, magnificent carriage and deportment - all these are signs of fine Bettas.

With the accumulation of mutant types and color combinations, intricate systems of classification and rules for judging have evolved. Several Betta specialty clubs are now in existence, including an International Betta Congress (IBC) which was organized in 1967. In 1969, the classifications in Betta shows were as follows:

Class A - Males. Dark-bodied types.
1. Red
2. Blue
3. Green
4. Open

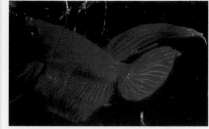

A dark-bodied red male. Photo by MP & C Piednoir.

A dark-bodied blue male. Photo by Kenjiro Tanaka.

A green male with split tail. Photo by Kenjiro Tanaka.

Two Cambodia males, light-bodied. Photo by Kenjiro Tanaka.

Magnificent male Betta with red fins and dark body. Photo by H.- J. Richter

Class B - Males. Light-bodied types.
1. Cambodia (Traditional)
2. Yellow
3. Open

Class C - Males. Both dark- and light-bodied types.
1. Butterflies (Fins have two distinct and clearly defined colors)
2. Multi-colors (Fish show three or more distinct colors)

Class D - Males. Provisional classes.
1. Blacks (melanos)
2. Double-tail (All colors)
3. Bi-color (A single, solid body color with a second, single color on the fins)

Above: The ideal Class C Butterflies. These are true Butterflies where the tips of the unpaired fins are pigmented. Photo by Kenjiro Tanaka. *Below:* A Class D male with a double-tail. Photo by Kenjiro Tanaka.

Class B male with a solid yellow body. Photo by Kenjiro Tanaka.

The trophy committee proudly displays their prizes at a local Siamese Fighting Fish show. These are NOT fighting competitions. The fish are judged on their beauty. Photo by S. Liebtrau.

A magnificent European strain with a golden body, a split tail and a blue dorsal. Photo by MP & C Piednoir.

A truly magnificent black (melano). Photo by Kenjiro Tanaka.

A beautiful twosome of blue-finned Cambodia with a split tail. Photo by Kenjiro Tanaka.

Class E - Females. All colors.

Bettas are usually exhibited in flat-sided "drum" bowls without plants or gravel. The bowls are shielded so that the fishes cannot see one another. The dividers are removed just prior to judging so that they will see their neighbors and be stimulated to display. Racks full of large, well developed Bettas in brilliant colors with perfect undamaged fins and in full display make a truly spectacular sight.

Judges look for small rips, missing scales or bent rays - any little flaw that could eliminate the entry - until at last one is named the champion. I do not know if wives have been lost at our kind of Betta contests. I do know that there can be no prouder owner than the one who carries home a trophy for his international champion Betta - and carries his beautiful Betta home with it.

Speaking of champions, if a champion aquarium fish of all time is ever crowned, in my opinion it will be a Betta.

COLOR AND GENETICS

The many beautiful color types available make Betta breeding a fascinating hobby. This is not a complicated task. With a little effort it is possible to understand the basic Betta colors and their various combinations. When these are understood, it is possible to set up crosses that will produce new color combinations, or to develop especially fine examples of some of the established types.

The most difficult thing when planning to breed for color is understanding the color-producing factors and considering them as separate elements. These will be described in a simplified "either-or" way. There are, of course, other details. For practical purposes I think that what is presented here will be enough.

Color may be present in its normal amount and distribution, or it may vary in several ways. If it varies, it can be absent, reduced in quantity or distribution, extended in quantity or distribution, or perhaps altered. In Betta coloration, each of the four color elements can vary these four ways, making it theoretically possible to come up with 256 different color combinations. No wonder there are so many color types!

It will be helpful to consider the basic color elements as I described them for the wild type Betta and then compare the condition of any given fish for each color element. For example, a fish that is "deep purple" can be more accurately described as having normal black pigment cells (melanophores), an extension of red color to cover the entire fish, an extension of the "sheen" in its blue variation, and no visible change as far as yellow color is concerned. The eye sees all of this as one, and the fish "looks" purple because it is viewed simultaneously as dark, red, and blue.

The following pages present brief summaries of what is known at this time about Betta genetics. While details are limited, they should be a guide to help the beginner make reasonably reliable predictions as to what to expect from a given mating.

Gene symbols

I have provided appropriate genetic symbols for each variation. These are used in the conventional way. For example, cc=Cambodia, Cc=mixed, appearing dark, and CC=dark (or normal). Upper-case letters signify complete or partial dominance and lower-case letters recessiveness.

Variation in black coloration

Domestic Bettas clearly demonstrate three types of color variation involving black pigmentation, each of which has been studied genetically. Each seems to be the result of a single gene mutation inherited in simple Mendelian fashion.

1. Cambodia

This is the nearest to a genetic "albino" in Bettas. Most or all of the integumentary (skin) melanin is absent. The name "Cambodia" apparently originated with Mr. Frank Locke of San Francisco, California. Upon seeing these light-colored fish in an import shipment, he thought they were Bettas of an unknown species.

Above: This young male shows no color in the fins and a pure cream on the body. Below: The Cambodia-type Betta shown here is hardly a gorgeous specimen but its colors are so pure it won a prize. Photos by Andre Roth.

He gave them a new scientific name. This name became so widely accepted that it still persists today. The gene responsible for the abnormality is recessive to the normal pigment-producing gene and is aptly symbolized "c" (the first letter of the name "Cambodia"). The fact that the "c" is lower-case shows that it is recessive. In order to show this abnormality, a Betta would have to receive a "c" gene from both of its parents. Otherwise, the fish would have normal melanin pigment and be dark.

2. Blond

This is the second genetic mutation that affects melanin production. This mutant does produce melanophores, but they are present in noticeably reduced numbers. The overall effect is a somewhat lighter body, clearly unlike Cambodia. The fish are usually taken for light-colored, normal fish. The most striking examples of "Blond" exist in reds. The red color may appear deep, blood red in fish with normal melanophores, but it will appear bright, brilliant scarlet when the Blond factor minimizes black.

However, the mutation probably has little if anything to do directly with red pigmentation. It is inherited as a simple Mendelian recessive. It is treated genetically like, but independent of, Cambodia.

The mutant was first described by Dr. Henry Wallbrunn. He named it "Bright" because of the way it affected the appearance of red. He designated it by the symbol "b." Since it actually may create different effects in blues, greens, and other colors without actually making them all "bright," I prefer the name "Blond." This name was used by Dr. Myron Gordon, who may have misinterpreted Dr. Wallbrunn's symbols.

An ideal Butterfly male Cambodia teasing a split-tail Cambodia. Photo by Kenjiro Tanaka.

Above: This is a beautiful double-tailed Blond. Below: A fully finned Blond with long fins. Photo by Kenjiro Tanaka.

The Melano Betta at its best! Photo by Kenjiro Tanaka.

The black on the body of this Cambodia is as intense as black can be. Photo by Kenjiro Tanaka.

This is a champion extended red Betta. Photo by Kenjiro Tanaka.

3. Melano

A third mutation alters the black color in Bettas. This time by apparently increasing it. I have suggested using the term "Melano" (symbolized by "m") since fish of this type would be considered melanistic (darker than normal), but not actually black. My data indicates that it is recessive to normal. Thus, it may be treated genetically like the previous mutants. The physiology of the variation is not clear, but the fish having the proper genetic type have very dark bodies and nearly black fins. The best colored fish seem to lack red. This indicates that black cells may completely obscure red or, possibly, red may somehow be converted to black.

I find that hobbyists have a great deal of trouble determining which genetic type they have, especially where black is concerned. A fish may be genetically the melanistic type and at the same time Cambodia or Blond - possibly both! This could account for the many "pale" blacks or odd-colored Cambodias with charcoal coloring in the fins. The pigment-forming systems of the fish may be antagonistically trying to increase black color on the one hand and decrease it on the other. It seems wisest to avoid using Cambodia or Blond stocks when working to improve Melano coloration.

Melanos display an additional genetic feature known as pleiotropism. This means that there are effects other than the primary one, apparently caused by the same mutation. In Melanos, this is infertility of females. Up until this time, no melanistic strain has been established that has fertile females. The stock must be maintained by crossing Melano males, which are fertile, to normal-appearing females that have one Melano gene. The offspring of such matings will include Melanos. The females may be obtained from crosses between Melano males and normal females.

Variation in red coloration

Probably the widest range of color variation among Bettas involves red. I have attempted to make a usable classification of these variations, none of which has appeared previously in the scientific literature.

This is about as black as a Betta can get without having cancer (melanoma).

A so-called *Halfmoon Turquoise.* Photo by Rajiv Masillamoni

One of the early blacks initially developed by Dr. Eduard Schmidt-Focke.

This is a Cambodia but it is so light in color that the trade calls it a *white*. Photo by Edward Taylor.

A variegated, mottled male Cambodia Betta. Photo by Kenjiro Tanaka.

A bad specimen of a Double-tailed Cambodia male. Photo by Kenjiro Tanaka.

The results of my genetic experiments thus far seem to indicate that several separate genes affect the development of red pigment.

1. Non-red

Some Bettas simply do not develop any red pigment. Although this type may be confused with another that I shall mention, it appears that the true Non-reds may be considered as having recessive genes that do not provide for normal development of red pigment. I symbolize the gene as "nr" and treat it as a simple Mendelian recessive in mating combinations involving red. Cambodia fish with the *nr* gene are often described as "White," "Cellophane," or given other descriptive names. They are most likely to be the ones taken to be albino.

2. Variegated fins

One of the most puzzling variations of red pigment is the type that develops in streaks and patterns in the fins, such as those popularly known as "Butterfly." The patterns are extremely variable, but fish may be classified as either solid or variegated. The variegation inheritance factors are interpreted somewhat as spotting patterns might be in dogs or other animals. More information is required, but at present I interpret this as the result of a dominant gene, symbolized "Vf," which controls the development in a special limited way.

In this case, it is not yet possible to make accurate predictions as to how many variegated fish might be obtained from a mating. Even if two variegated parents are used, there are likely to be a number of solid red-finned progeny. I have always been able to obtain some variegated finned fish from parents of this type. An interesting, but possibly confusing, aspect of this variation in expression of the gene is that it apparently responds to selection; that is, if progressively lighter fish are selected for breeders, it may be possible to eventually obtain some fish with no red at all. These fish would look exactly like the Non-reds, but Non-reds breed true. These fish always produce progeny with variegated fins or even normal solid-colored fins, and only a few without red.

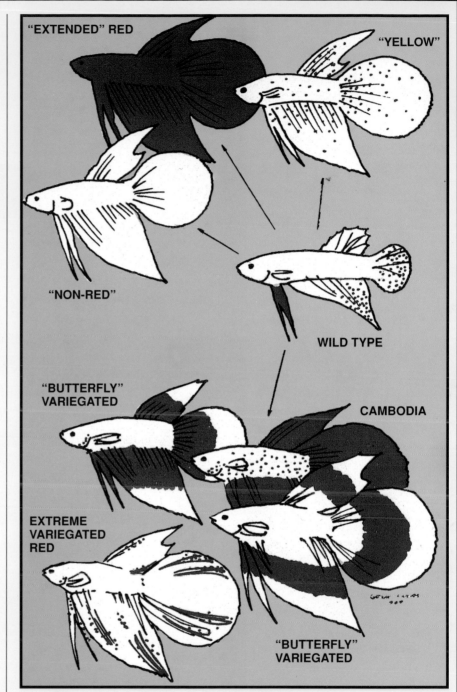

Variation of red pigment development.

3. Extended red

A third genetic variation involving red is an increased intensity and distribution of it, especially into the body. Wild fish normally have red only in the fins and on a small patch at the rear edge of the gill cover. My experiments indicate that the extension may be caused by a dominant gene, which I symbolize as "R" for red because these fish are the ones that are noticeably red. My fish of this type have always produced at least some similar progeny. Like variegation, this trait seems to respond to selection. It is possible to produce very intense red color with a well-managed breeding program.

An interesting side effect involving red is that it seems to be influenced by sex. Females are ordinarily somewhat less affected than males. It may require diligent effort

to produce good-colored red females. The red also varies considerably in intensity depending upon the genetic type of black the fish has. Cambodias with extended red may look peach-colored or light red. Blond types are generally the most brilliant red. Fish with normal amounts of black pigment are a deep blood red or maroon color.

I have been unable to detect anything that looks like a general reduction of

red similar to the Blond expression of black. I do have a suspicion that the yellow in what we ordinarily think of as yellow Bettas may in fact be improperly developed red. The patterns of yellow appear to duplicate red patterns in most cases.

Variations in yellow coloration

While there are definitely yellow Bettas, I have been unable to

Short-finned Cambodias. These fish are true butterflies with the outside edges of the unpaired fins being pigmented while the bases are not. Photo by Kenjiro Tanaka.

A truly magnificent mottled Cambodia Double-tail. Photo by Kenjiro Tanaka.

determine that there are any genes that just make a Betta yellow. This may seem confusing, but the effect can be adequately explained by considering that fish could have combinations of other genes that remove black and red, leaving what are essentially colorless fish. They may or may not have sheen. I consider them to be Cambodia and Non-red. In this state they may be called "Cellophane" if they are nearly transparent. At present, I believe it possible that strongly colored yellows are fish that would be very red if they could develop red pigment. Further analysis is necessary, but at least I have been able to produce Cambodia Non-red progeny from other stocks which look identical to "yellow." I consider this fairly good evidence that my interpretation is correct. Also, since the two suggested genes are recessive, they should breed true. I have always found this to be the case. Until additional information accumulates to prove otherwise, I recommend considering yellow as the above combinations.

Variations in green-blue "metallic sheen" coloration

I think the most striking variations in Bettas are those with the metallic sheens—blues and greens. They are unusual and brilliant colors compared to the others. They also are produced in an entirely different way since they are not pigments, but physical phenomena that modify or are modified by the true pigmentary colors. As mentioned previously, they are apparently produced by light being scattered through tiny, possibly colorless, crystals, principally located in cells called guanophores or iridocytes. The color effect is created in much the same way as the blue of the sky; the tiny particles scatter the light to create a bluish color. The presence of black pigment cells makes the blue deeper, and the presence of some element of yellow —possibly in the slime layer—probably makes the blue look green. Whatever the case may be, the expression of this characteristic is quite variable and capable of producing some fantastic color effects.

At this time there are just two mutant genes known that affect iridocyte color. One changes the color itself and the other extends it over significantly more of the surface of the fish. The two are described here.

1. Blue
Since the iridocyte color in the spots and stripes of wild fish is green, it is logical that the blue must be the abnormal variation. This gene has been known for a long

time, but by other names. These names are inappropriate in genetic terminology since they suggest that green is the abnormal condition. The Blue and Green types were described by Goodrich and Mercer in 1934, but they have no information regarding inheritance. The name *viridens* (symbol "V") was given to the green

The blue is metallic in this strain of short-finned Betta. Photo by Kenjiro Tanaka.

variation by Eberhardt in 1941. It was called Green (symbolized "G") by Wallbrunn in 1948. I have suggested calling the gene Blue (symbolized "B1"), since it is my judgment that blue is the abnormal condition. The capitalized symbol indicates dominance. In this case, it is a special form that geneticists call

incomplete or partial dominance. When one "blue gene" is present, the fish is blue. If it receives "blue genes" from both parents, it will still be blue, but a different color blue. These two blue colors are generally referred to as Blue (often called Cornflower, Bright, Intermediate, etc.) and Steel Blue. Green and Steel Blue will breed true, while the Blue cannot. It is possible to obtain all Blue spawns by mating Greens with Steel Blues, thus producing progeny all possessing one normal and one mutant (Blue) gene.

2. Spread iridocytes
Another variation, known for some time but extremely variable and

poorly understood, is the one that noticeably increases the distribution of the blue or green metallic sheen. My interpretation of the abnormality again depends on comparing it to the wild type. Wild fish have this color only on spots on the scales and streaks in the fins. Domestic fish are often almost entirely covered with it. In highly colored examples, only the head, gill covers, and usually the paired fins lack sheen.

Although it is difficult to determine, because of the variability of development, there seems to be a gene responsible for the increase. This behaves as a genetic dominant. Eberhardt described the two alternatives in 1941, symbolizing them as "ri" (reduced iridocytes) and "Ri." In present terminology, "Ri" indicates that the wild type was abnormal. I use the alternative symbol "Si" for spread iridocytes, since it appropriately designates the abnormal condition and indicates its dominance.

The spread condition, as I have already indicated, is highly variable. The fish may be nearly covered with sheen or it may be

Metallic blue strain of Betta. Photo by Kenjiro Tanaka.

Old style of blue Betta without the emphasis of the metallic scales. Photo by Karl Knaack.

A blue Double-tail. Photo by Kenjiro Tanaka.

A diagrammatic melanophore (black color cell in the skin) showing how the expansion and contraction can affect the color of the fish. Drawn by Gene Lucas.

spread, but with "thin" places on various parts of the fins. The very dense coating may almost completely cover color that lies underneath, such as red. If so, it may be difficult to see what red the fish actually has. The "thin" places, especially in the fins, may allow red to show through so that the fins are often red-green, red-blue, green-red, or blue-red. The color appears to blend as a wash rather than to be sharply defined as is the red when variegated.

Odd or poorly understood variations

There are a few color variations that are repeatedly observed, but whose genetic background is unclear. They may be non-genetic, but information is inconclusive at this time. If genetic, the genetic

mechanism is far from clear.

1. Opaque

A peculiar factor causes the deposit of a creamy-looking substance throughout the skin of the fish. It is even found infiltrating the eyes. It appears to accumulate gradually and, as the fish grows older, it may cause a rather unpleasant thickening of the skin. Pop-eye seems to be highly prevalent in these fish, possibly because of the accumulated material. It has not been analyzed chemically, but it does have a distinct color that is independent of other color elements. It tends to make Cambodia fish look whitish, and it appears as a sort of creamy wash through greens, blues, and reds. The entire effect is rather ghostly. If it is genetic, it

is apparently inherited as a dominant or incomplete dominant. I symbolized it as "Op" for opaque. This seems to be an aptly descriptive—if not spectacular—name.

2. Color loss

A trait that might appropriately be called pied or piebald involves the loss of pigments. There is some evidence that it may be genetic, but examples are often isolated and cannot be obtained predictably. I am reluctant to call them pied, because what appears to happen is that their pigments begin to disappear. What is most unique about this loss is that different pigments may disappear or regenerate independently. They also may regenerate at a later time, again independently.

There is no doubt that the appearance of the fish is modified. Some that are affected are very striking; others look pretty bad. I have one strain that seems to lose black pigment around the head. This makes the fish look curiously like miniature white-faced cattle. Because the genetic evidence is so questionable, I have not attempted to make a

This blond or Cambodia is blotched with interesting markings and a lovely double tail. But it has no category in the show except the Miscellaneous class.

symbolic designation for the condition.

Genetic variations other than color

There are two obvious structural variations in domestic Bettas. One is so common and well-known that it is no longer considered a variation. The other is rapidly becoming well-known because it is so distinctive, although it is still relatively rare.

1. Prachtiges (from a German word meaning, roughly, splendid)

More commonly known as the Veil-tail or Long-fin variety. Almost all domestic Bettas are of this genetic type. It was probably discovered and developed long ago by Siamese breeders. We know that when Bettas were imported into the United States in 1927, Veil-tails were already highly developed.

The name was provided by Eberhardt in 1941. His data was limited, as mine is. However, all indications are that the variation is genetic and functions as a dominant to the normal, short-fined condition of the wild type. In this case, Eberhardt's symbol "P" is correctly applied according to modern practice. Therefore, I believe it should stand unchanged.

2. Double-tail

The most distinctive mutant in Bettas, in my opinion, is the Double-tail. It has also been

Almost a true Butterfly, but magnificently colored red anyway.

Most Cambodias show red; this blond shows blue. Photo by Kenjiro Tanaka.

Two male Double-tail Cambodias showing different colorations. Photo by Kenjiro Tanaka.

Wow! This champion has black fins on a turquoise body and a double tail fin. Photo by Kenjiro Tanaka.

referred to as the Split-tail. I think this designation causes confusion between the real mutant and a condition that can occur in normal fish. Ordinarily, tails may split and resemble the tail of the Doubles, at least superficially.

The Double-tail has a double caudal peduncle. From this grow two separate tailfins, one above the other. The rays in each "lobe" of the tail will number eight or ten. In a normal single-lobed tail, there are only ten or twelve rays. The dorsal fin is also a noticeable feature; it may contain up to three times the number of rays found in a normal dorsal. The Double-tail dorsal may be larger than the anal fin in development and ray number. The body is usually shorter and thicker, often unattractive. I have observed several that had at least two extra rows of scales. Since I have started crossing them with other strains, I am getting more attractive body shapes and more colors. All the color types found in normal Bettas should eventually be available in Double-tails, greatly increasing the assortment of Betta types.

The various colors and fin shapes is, of course, merely a series of abnormalities. Fortunately, they are attractive abnormalities. But this monster has lost the top half of his tail and caudal peduncle and the lower half of the tail seems to be merging with the anal fin. Fortunately, this fish was not used as the basis of a new strain. Photo by Kenjiro Tanaka.

The Double-tail is inherited as a genetic recessive and it is symbolized as "dt." I predict a rewarding future for this unusual form.

Miscellaneous abnormalities

A number of characteristics commonly observed in Bettas are thought to be "bad." Hence, breeders do not ordinarily breed from individuals with these deformities. I refer to such defects as missing pelvic fins, curved or misaligned fin rays, and similar abnormalities. Most of these impair the looks of the fish, but at this time there is no evidence that any of them are genetic. I have deliberately mated fish lacking pelvic fins without obtaining any abnormal offspring. I feel that these fish may be used for breeding if they have other known genetic traits that are desirable.

Over the years, an assortment of physical and pigmental variations has developed in Goldfish. This certainly resulted in an increased demand. As a result of the development of many new and exotic types, I predict a like future for the Bettas.

HEALTH

Unfortunately, not too much is known about specific Betta diseases. To my knowledge, no special research has been carried out on them. Some research has been done on the diseases of aquarium fish in general. In this chapter I discuss the more common of those which also affect Bettas.

Oodinium (Velvet)

One of the most common ailments of aquarium fishes is called white spot disease, or ich, after the protozoan *Ichthyophthirius multifiliis*, which causes it. It is characterized by fine white spots which cover the victim. Bettas seldom suffer from ich, but they do fall victim to a disease often mistaken for it: *Oodinium (=Amyloodinium)*, commonly known as Velvet. It is the Betta's nemesis.

Like ich, it is a protozoan. Its life cycle is not too different from that of *Ichthyophthirius*. *Oodinium*, though, in both the parasitic and free-swimming forms, is capable of performing photosynthesis. The free-swimming form is dependent upon this for nourishment, although the parasitic form probably derives most of its nourishment from the host fish. It is recommended that the tank be darkened as an aid to breaking the life cycle by inhibiting the development of the intermediate stage.

When the organism attaches itself to a fish in sufficient numbers, the fish soon becomes listless. It clamps its fins and wastes away. The organism is hard to see on light-colored fishes, but dark fishes seem to be covered with a light tan or golden haze-like dust. I have observed the organisms, which in the attached state resemble simple stalks with tannish "spores" (resembling a fungus), in clumps all over the fish, even in the gill chambers and the mouth. I have even observed what I thought were spores inside dissected specimens, although I cannot be positive of this. The organism apparently multiplies inside this sporelike structure. The structure eventfully falls off and releases swarms of the new generation. These swarms then reinfect their host or some other fish.

Oodinium seems to infect only certain species. For example, when I first encountered it, it killed a dozen female Bettas in a community tank without harming any of the other fish. It is especially hard on Bettas. It causes a high mortality rate. It will wipe out a spawn of fry in a few days once it gets started. Its worst feature is that the fry are usually too far gone before the breeder realizes that something is wrong.

Possibly the stronger fish can resist the organism, or water conditions may retard its development. When lightly infected fishes are put into new water or a spawning tank, the protozoans develop rapidly and the infection becomes obvious.

The most effective control seems to be copper. Malachite green and methylene blue, available in most pet shops, are moderately effective. Should the Bettas become listless or sluggish, remove the copper and change part of the water. When the fish look normal for a

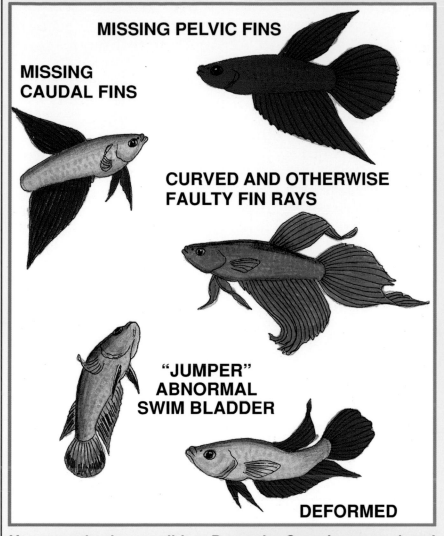

MISSING PELVIC FINS

MISSING CAUDAL FINS

CURVED AND OTHERWISE FAULTY FIN RAYS

"JUMPER" ABNORMAL SWIM BLADDER

DEFORMED

Non-genetic abnormalities. Drawn by Gene Lucas; colored by John Quinn.

week or so, the copper may be removed. The gradual increase in copper may itself create problems eventually.

All fish, even those not obviously infected, should be treated. The containers and all other paraphernalia that come into contact with the fish should be treated also. Care should be taken not to transfer the parasites from the old container to the new one by using contaminated nets or other equipment.

Fungus

Bettas seem more prone than most fish to fin damage resulting from fungoid or bacterial infections. I know of no study of Bettas that has identified the specific organisms involved in these infections, but they are probably the same ones that infect other fishes. The problem is undoubtedly related to the long, delicate finnage and the mode of culture of the fish. "Bad" water probably tends to weaken the fish or the fins, and thus lower the general resistance.

The infection is detected by the presence of a fuzzy growth, or the disappearance of pigment and fragmentation of fin material. Holes or splits appear, and sometimes large portions of the fin appear to decay and fall off. The recommended treatment for these problems is better care and conditioning, supplemented by fungicides or antibiotic treatments available in aquarium pet shops.

The so-called "mouth fungus" is not really a fungus at all. It is a slime bacterium. The lips of the infected fish turn white. In severe cases, the mouth appears to be plugged with cotton. This disease is highly infectious and often does great damage in tanks crowded with females or young. The most specific treatment is one of the "mycins" or "cyclines" (such as aureomycin or tetracycline). The accepted dose is 25 to 50 milligrams per gallon of water. They usually come in 250 mg capsules that can be pulled or cut open. The powder should be dissolved in lukewarm water and then added directly to the tank.

Pop-eye

"Pop-eye" is a recurring problem in Bettas. There may be several causes, such as infectious organisms or poor conditions; some, on the other hand, are apparently related to genetic susceptibility. Again I would recommend better care and conditioning, supplemented by antibiotic treatments. I am not specifying which antibiotics, since several may be effective. Broad spectrum types, such as tetracycline, are probably the most helpful.

One Betta mutant suffers Pop-eye as a side effect to an unusual pigment deposit. In this case, I suspect the problem is the result of an inherited metabolic disturbance for which little can be done.

Tumors

Bettas also may be affected by tumors, but I have rarely seen one. I consider them a minor problem. Real tumors, if they are cancerous, are probably not worth treating, since treatment may be difficult and, more often than not, useless. Since strain differences exist in other animals, it is quite possible that "tumor-prone" strains also develop in fishes. If this tendency appears in any stock, I would call it to the attention of someone interested in fish pathology, and I would not use that stock for routine breeding.

Dropsy

An abnormality that seems to occur more frequently in Bettas than in many other species of fishes is dropsy. The tissues fill with fluid, and as they become distended the scales protrude in a characteristic fashion. Ordinarily, the problem is due to kidney or circulatory malfunction and is likely to be fatal. Sometimes excess fluids can be extracted from the abdominal cavity with a hypodermic syringe, but usually this gives only temporary relief. If the problem is the result of kidney infection, antibiotic treatment may help. At any rate, it is worth trying.

Larger parasites

Although the special culture techniques for Bettas minimize the possibility, they also can become victims of large, external parasites, such as anchor worms, fish lice, flukes, and the like. These can be treated by picking off the offender with tweezers and touching the wound with a drop of mercurochrome.

Injuries

Scale losses or fin damage from fighting will usually take care of themselves if the weakened fish are allowed to rest and are given good care while they recuperate.

Generally speaking

It should be obvious that Betta ailments are similar to those that affect other aquarium fishes. Certain infections can cause captive Bettas more damage because of their peculiar living conditions. Optimum care and conditioning will prevent most problems before they arise. In some cases, however, the only remedy will be to isolate or destroy the sick fish before it infects others.

BREEDING BETTAS

The mating of domestic Bettas has been described by many breeders, most of whose procedures are similar. Neither the size of the breeding tank nor the water depth appears to be critical. I successfully have raised spawns in water depths ranging from one to sixteen inches. Most breeders use a three- to five-gallon tank.

Light, temperature, and furnishings

Bettas prefer slightly warmer water than most aquarium fishes. 80° F seems to be optimal. Four to five degrees above or below this, breeding activity falls off rapidly. Their tolerance of pH and hardness range is considerable. However, I find a pH of 6-7 to be best, along with water that is on the "soft" side.

I do not use plants, gravel, rocks, or even filters in spawning tanks. The fry are very tiny and I like to be able to watch their early progress.

The amount and type of light can vary as long as it is enough for the fish to see. Because eggs and fry might suffocate if the guardian male cannot see to keep them in the bubble nest, many breeders provide continuous light for the first few days.

I prefer not to keep snails with my Bettas. Large Bettas will kill them. Also, they are a nuisance in fry tanks, which I siphon frequently, because they plug siphon hoses.

are willing to breed. However, the younger fish generally spawn more readily.

The nest

The male, when properly stimulated by the sight of a desirable female, will begin to construct a nest of small bubbles (about 1/8 inch

Because the female bettas are much less combative than the males, numbers of them can be maintained in the same tank with only occasional squabbling and no great damage. Photo by H. J. Richter.

Selecting breeders

Breeders are selected on the basis of genetic traits—coloration or whatever other characteristics the breeder may be interested in developing. The age of the fish is not important as long as they

in diameter), which may be one to many layers thick. The nest may be small or large; size is not important. It may be built anywhere in the tank, but if an object, such as a floating leaf or a heater tube, is present, it will probably be built under it or anchored to it. Some breeders place artificial materials, such as pieces of plastic, halved styrofoam cups, squares of waxed paper, etc., in the water. The fish almost always build their nests under these objects. In fact, this often stimulates reluctant nest builders.

Pairing

The fish may be introduced into the breeding tank at the same time but kept separated by a glass partition. Or, the female can be placed in a small glass container set inside the tank. A quart jar is good for this; a breeding trap also might be used. A glass chimney from a kerosene lamp is ideal, since it can be lifted to free the female without unduly disturbing the fish or the nest. I usually leave the empty container in the tank for the female to hide behind if the male attacks her too vigorously.

While the male is building the nest, he will pause to "flirt" with the female by flaring his fins, batting his tail, and wagging his body. When she is ready to receive him, the female will flush intensively and show dark, vertical bands

Above: The red male Betta builds his bubblenest as soon as he sees a female. Frequently, even when kept alone and with no female in sight, the male will build a bubblenest. Photo by Hans Joachim Richter. *Below:* Once the bubblenest is built, the male will go after the female. Usually she is battered a bit before she gives in to the spawning urge. If she isn't ready to spawn she might be killed by the male. Photo by Hans Joachim Richter.

while swimming on the side of her container nearest him. When this happens they may be put together.

His excitement rises to fever pitch when he realizes that she is within reach. With fins stretched taut, he wigwags his body in front of her, then swims off a few inches, inviting her to follow. It is also quite normal for the male to intersperse these invitations with aggressive overtures, often nipping at her fins or scales. If she is receptive, she will display in response and soon follow him under the nest. Here the mating will proceed. If not, she may flee and be pursued and attacked. If not removed, she may be injured or killed.

Egglaying

The mating itself is an interesting ritual consisting of a series of embraces. The male usually turns on his side and lets his head and tail droop toward the bottom, forming an inverted "U." The female turns on her back and nestles in this fold, lying at cross angles to him. The vents of the two are then close together and the eggs and milt (containing sperm) are emitted simultaneously. Fertilization is external.

The embraces last 15-20 seconds. They are repeated many times over a three or four hour period. During the first few tries, there may be no eggs released; then a few will appear. At the peak of the spawning, the number may go to 20 or 30 per embrace. This tapers off until finally there will be none. The total may reach a thousand or more, but usually there are only a few hundred. Large females that have not spawned recently can be expected to produce the greatest number of eggs. Kept at 80°F, females may be ready to spawn again in a week. Males can be spawned almost daily for short periods of time. No records are available, but we can assume that excessive mating could result in at least a temporary decrease in male fertility.

After each embrace, during which the eggs are released, the usual routine is for the female to move away while the male picks up the eggs and places them in the bubble nest. Females occasionally help with this, or they may ignore or eat the eggs.

Above: The female joins the male under his bubblenest and he wraps his body about hers. The first few attempts of body wrapping are usually futile, but eventually they line up their genital pores and spawning commences. Photo by Hans Joachim Richter.
Below: Spawning lasts about 20 seconds per embrace with the entire process lasting an hour or so. Once spawning is completed and the female does not approach the male any more, she should be removed or the male might attack her. Photo by Hans Joachim Richter.

Sometimes males will eat eggs, but this is unusual. Once the spawning is completed, the male begins to attend the nest. He may then attack and drive the female away since he has no further need of her. Since small tanks do not give the female room to escape, she should be removed before she is injured. The male may even be so aggressive that she must be removed before spawning is completed, but that is no great loss. I find it difficult to rear large spawns anyway, since they require a great deal of space, food, and care. I would much rather rear 50 or 100 good fish from a spawn than 500 that are inferior.

Hatching

The fry hatch in 36 to 48 hours even though their development is not complete. They are unable to do much more than wiggle, and they often wiggle themselves free of the bubbles. They cannot make coordinated movements, but spurt about the tank, eventually settling to the bottom. During this period, the father is kept busy rebuilding the nest and replacing the sinking fry. Good males have great patience and work constantly at this task. I have seen some work diligently for several consecutive days and nights without "sleep" with no apparent ill effects.

After a day or so the fry reach the free-swimming stage. They will be observed all over the tank, lying horizontally just below the surface. Since the paternal instinct of the male may become exhausted and he may begin to regard his offspring as food, it is best to remove him from the tank at this time. I have left males with fry for as long as five or six weeks and had no problems. However, I do not recommend it.

Baby feeding

Once the fry are free-swimming, there are only a few simple rules to follow. The most important is to supply adequate food. I believe that far and away the most significant factor in fry loss is starvation. I find it a simple matter to culture them once one gets the hang of it.

Protozoan "starter" cultures may be purchased from biological supply houses or obtained from generous biology teachers.

Above: As spawning embraces continue they become more and more perfect with the couple in a tight embrace and rolling over. After the embrace, the female is usually paralyzed for 5-10 seconds to give the male a chance to gather up the eggs. Photo by Hans Joachim Richter.
Below: While the females floats away paralyzed, the male scoops up the falling eggs in his mouth and blows them into the bubblenest. By the time he has done this, the female regains consciousness and is ready to continue the process. Photo by Hans Joachim Richter.

Cultures also may be started with tank water, particularly water from filter boxes. I culture protozoans in quart jars. My method is simple. I assume that the starting culture has very few organisms in it. I fill it with newly aged water and add an alfalfa pellet, a rabbit food pellet, and a dried bean or pea. As these begin to decompose, they provide food for bacteria and other microscopic organisms. The bacteria themselves may serve as food for the protozoans.

The culture may take a week or more to build up. Once it does, the organisms will be so plentiful they can be observed as "dust particles" in the water. They can best be seen against a dark background with a flashlight beamed through the culture. To feed, put a third or half of one of these jars into the spawning tank. Use a flashlight to check the tank. When there are only a few protozoans left, pour in a batch from another jar so that the fry can feed continuously. Refill the jars with fresh aged water. In a day or so, they will be ready to use again. If the cultures become unproductive, more pellets should be added and the water renewed.

Sometimes the cultures become so bacteria-laden that protozoans never start to develop. Bad cultures usually can be detected by strong odors and cloudy water. Good cultures smell very little, sometimes not at all. Never put smelly cultures into the fry tank. Fry cannot eat bacteria and the bacteria may consume large amounts of oxygen, causing the fry to suffocate. When cultures heavily populated with protozoans are no longer needed, they may be allowed to dry out, saved, and restarted at any time by just adding water and food.

Some breeders believe that fry get off to a good start if newly hatched (less than 24 hours) brine shrimp are fed from the beginning. Micro-pulverized dry foods, paste foods, and hardboiled egg yolk are other first foods often used. I start by feeding protozoans. Only after three or four days do I gradually introduce brine shrimp. A few days later, I stop offering protozoans and depend completely on brine shrimp. From then on the fry are never

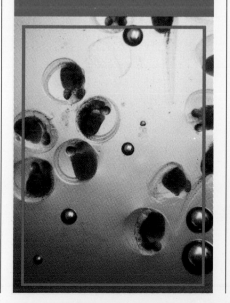

Above: A closeup of the male, the bubblenest and the hundreds of babies in his care. As the fry fall out of the nest, the male spits them back encased in a bubble. Photo by Hans Joachim Richter. *Below:* A photomicrograph of the developing Betta eggs.

without them. Even when they are mature enough to eat other foods, I always offer my Bettas brine shrimp every few days.

Fry grow rapidly if they are fed properly and not crowded. Some precocious individuals may grow faster than, and attempt to eat, some of their siblings. These should be removed and jarred. Spawns can be separated into size groups and distributed to several tanks for optimum growth and survival.

Suffocation

Next to starvation, suffocation is probably the biggest problem encountered when raising fry. Most breeders do not filter new fry tanks, since the filter may filter out fry and food. As a result, scums may form on the surface and interfere with air exchange. I usually put a small air hose in the tank and allow it to bubble slowly. This may help aerate the water, but it is probably more important for breaking up any surface film.

There is a popular belief that, unless the tank is covered, the air above the water may be cool, and that this will in some way injure the fry, particularly during the stage of labyrinth development. In my experience, this is not a major cause of fry mortality. I think that if adequate food and oxygen are available, fry will get along fine with no special care other than routine maintenance. This is simply to hold water temperature at around 80°F., and to siphon and replace part of the water on a regular basis as soon as the fry are large enough to escape siphoning.

In conclusion

I hope the information provided in this book will help the budding "Bettaphile" know more about his Bettas and lead to successful and rewarding experiences with them. Bettas are tough, adaptable, and relatively undemanding. I think they deserve recognition as one of the finest of aquarium fishes.

Probably being the most colorful freshwater fish, being easy to keep, having interesting spawning habits and being inexpensive to buy and maintain, have made Siamese Fighting Fish among the ten most popular fishes of the thousands available to hobbyists